juxtaposition

Kristen Spaulding

BookLeaf Publishing

India | USA | UK

Presentation by *BookLeaf Publishing*

Web: www.bookleafpub.com

E-mail: info@bookleafpub.com

ISBN: 9789363318007

First edition 2024

Eugene,

Thank you for your love and optimism.

Mildred

PREFACE

losing through you what seemed myself;
i find selves unimaginably mine; beyond
sorrow's own joys and hoping's very fears

yours is the light by which my spirit's born:
yours is the darkness of my soul's return
—you are my sun, my moon, and all my stars

e.e cummings

twenty-three (2013)

you don't know the burning feeling
you cause every time we speak.
this burn in my eyes, my nose, my heart...
i don't understand it any more than you do.

so when you thank me for thinking of
your grandfather in critical condition,
while I know she's hardly aware, hardly
concerned
the blood becomes hot in my veins.

and I hate her, all of her... her full ride to college,
rock climbing, horseback riding, artistic
perfection
seems to me garbage, if she doesn't appreciate
the gift that is you.

(a gift i always seek, but never receive
like a child on christmas, confused,
because she tried her best to be good)

wilder mind (2017)

does anybody else
hear that wild whisper calling?
in the middle of the night,
my wilder mind just can't stop running.

toward that place i've never been,
to the people we might be,
if you're out there, just say anything,
say it's not just me.

does anybody else
flirt with the melancholy?
in the middle of the night,
my wilder mind goes willingly

toward that memory of you,
to the life we never built,
if you're out there, just say anything
i'm lost beneath this guilt.

it's the never feeling finished,
it's that line of questioning.
it's the wondering where you are,
and if you ever think of me.

origin story

I am from a world of distinctive colors,
The ratty burnt orange computer chair,
The "country blue" recliner in the living room
corner,
The yellow Kool Aid mixing spoon with the tip
dyed red.

I am from twenty minutes outside Atlanta,
where bustling city and southern country meet.
I am from a rickety metal swing set and a
blue baby pool we'd use when there wasn't a
drought.

I am from Katbird and Max-a-Million,
In the middle of Amanda Joy Lowe and
Ambergini.
I am from the Sunday lunches at Aunt Donna's,
And from picking out food at the free pantry.

I am from the pot we boiled water in when the
gas was off,
from the sleeping bags we burrowed in on nights
without heat.
I am from the basements and guest bedrooms we
occupied
while "in between houses right now."

I am from the Toy Story VHS Dad spent his last
$20 on.
I am from lying on my bedroom floor by the
radio,
listening to Radio Disney down low
so he wouldn't hear my devil's music.

I am from the happier "Who left the barn door
open?"
And "You make a better door than you do a
window."
But also from the "Stop crying or I'll give you
something to cry about"
And the "You've got the devil in you."

I am from chaos and fear,
I am from love and warmth,
I am from strength and sorrow.
I am from juxtaposition.

phantom threats, forever

how does one
grow up and stop
listening for
how hard the door shut
how heavily the footsteps fell
how loudly the dishes slammed
and every way
the words rose
and fell,
the eyes slit
and shifted?

my dad is dying

another weekend phone call,
another half hour spent
lying motionless on the couch,
processing it all
while I listen to my daughter
squealing happily elsewhere
with her father.

the talk of new pain meds,
wheelchairs, oxygen;
then comes that phrase
I've heard you mention
a couple of times now
"I have a feeling the whole family
needs to come this time."

Cancer on Father's Day

Sweat is beading on your brow,
You stop to find your breath.
Someone finds a subject change.
It hurts to think of death.

But every visit is laced with pain
And sneaking photographs,
And saying one simple good-bye
Becomes the most difficult task.

Will we see your face again?
Will we hear your laugh?
Do you still have stories to share,
Or will this one be the last?

Is being positive just being naive?
Is fearing the worst being dark?
I'm not ready for you to leave,
When I've just now opened my heart.

doubt

Whispers of
ghosts past…
of infidelity,
of doubt,
(of not being sure
about me
after so long)
are haunting from
the shadows
in the corner of
his room.
Why do I search
when I never like
what I find?
Slam the book closed.
Squeeze my eyes shut.
Cover my ears.
Trust the words
he says
and not the words
he wrote
when no one
was watching.

pathological

you lied about your sister,
you lied about my dad,
you lied about the photos,
but your lies were all i had.

you lied about your nephew,
you lied about the party,
you lied about the women,
and you were never really sorry.

you lied about the grocery store,
you lied about your friends,
you lied about those websites,
then you lied about our end.

she saved me

strawberry juice
staining your cheeks,
your knotted hair
pushed back.

mud on your hands,
determined eyes,
the twinkling sound
of your laugh.

you are nothing like
they said you'd be
and, my daughter,
i am so glad.

My Father's Daughter

I am my father's daughter,
My laugh booms loud and
Out of control
Like the funniest thing
In all human history
Has just been whispered
In my ear
And people stare.

I am my father's daughter,
I can work a crowd
And give a speech
And move your heart
To action
But you wonder when
I'll learn to be
more tactful and
Less bold.

I am my father's daughter,
I struggle to show
Gentleness
To those I love most
But slip a dollar in every
Beggar's cup

And think about them
The whole drive
Home.

I am my father's daughter,
There's a seed of anger
Deep in my belly
And I lashed out
Half my life
At those who dared
to cherish me
But I fought my demons harder
With courage I earned
from facing his.

I am my father's daughter,
He told me
a hundred times
About not knowing
The value of his father
Until the hour was
Too late
The time of death
Was called,
The moment gone.

I am my father's daughter,
I can't speak to what
I'm feeling

So I wrote it in a poem
I'll share with
Those I love
And wonder if
I'm a narcissist
Or just need someone
To see my heart
Without the nakedness
Of spoken words.

complicit

your parents were black and white,
and to them, it was bad enough
that you turned out grey.
so who the fuck was I?
with euphoric yellows,
tranquil blues, and fiery reds?
where did you find me,
some alley way? some charity shop?
they called for turpentine, and quick...
and though you weren't the one
to douse me in it, you surely looked away.

divorce

The strangest part
of this past year
was becoming
muted,
colors fading,
to almost nothing.
I remember
the younger me,
so vibrant.
I finally see how it happens.
We just get broken
down to silence,
down to agreeable gray.

adhd

a load of laundry left unstarted,
the open silverware drawer,
an important document lost,
a cabinet door left ajar.

the piles of papers i search,
a deadline i almost miss,
the gas tank on empty again,
a preschool dress-up day i forget.

a conversation i interrupt,
another thought that slips my mind,
the way i'm sure my boss noticed
that today i was running behind.

another doctor's office,
and imposter syndrome nerves.
i hope this time i see someone
who helps me feel i'm heard.

attention deficit, impulsive,
a hyperactive brain,
i know it's a disorder,
but that doesn't ease my shame.

you found me

the first night i encountered you,
i showed up skeptical, hollow, starved
for a bond i wasn't sure existed

i prepared for another helping
of the utter bullshit that kept leaving me
emptier with every endeavor.

but from the moment you sat down,
your eyes disarmed me and awoke some hope
that stirred fearfully from deep within.

we found a mutual kindness there,
a common thread of morals and wonderings,
an unexpected sameness in our souls.

you spoke with reckless abandon
of our chemistry, of subsequent dates, of flowers
you wondered whether you should have brought.

i watched you with a cautious smile,
wondering where you came from, where you've
been,
and how you found me after all this time.

hope

if this really is a dream,
i pray i never wake
as i've started to settle safely
into the idea that you'll stay.

it startles me to realize
(as I've done a thousand times)
that i almost lived and died
without ever feeling this way.

you

your kindness is
a treasure
i want to protect,
to return to you.

you afford grace,
you listen with love,
you do what you can
to make life better.

at every turn,
you deserve all of it back
(and more)

acceptance

there was a time
(many if i'm honest)
that i felt hunger was
the only thing sustaining me.

protruding bones and
rail thin arms were all that
gave me the sense
that i had a right to be here.

spots on my vision and
an irregular heart beat
were trophies to be collected
and treasured as the proof

the evidence that i could be
disciplined enough, thin enough
to deserve the space i took up
(it was small enough, after all)

and when boy after boy, man after man,
cheated and betrayed (always with someone
smaller),
i found only the extra bit of skin i pinched
between my fingers to hold accountable.

instead of blaming him, of blaming them,
i'd show them what they lost by
disappearing more, becoming less.
the next man wouldn't be tempted to stray.

but these days, my daughter lays her head
upon my rounded tummy like a pillow.
my lover takes a handful of my hips,
breathes a contented sigh.

and although there's so much more of me
to make peace with, perhaps to love,
i find myself more worthy, more beautiful now
than in the days of skin and bones.

wanted

though we share no genetic link,
(my body never carried yours)
it's hard to imagine that DNA
could make me love you any more.

for if i loved you any more than this,
it might split me right in two,
spilling out and covering us all
in a flood none could subdue.

your laugh, your spirit, your wit--
all treasure i hope you keep.
and when you grow, (please) always know
you were wanted beyond belief.

the gardener

little flower,
you started
as a seed
in my palm.

you might have
stayed tiny
and contained
forever,

but i chose you.
and that means
you needed me
to show up.

the soil,
the water,
the sun,
and the shade.

on good days
and bad,
rainy days,
and sweltering

i remembered you
each day,
and returned.
mostly because

you never
asked
to be planted
by me.

so i couldn't
bring myself
to let you
die.

and now
my friends
ooh and ahh
at your colors.

and i wonder
how much sooner
we'd have grown
with more care.

Kieran

there are a few lessons i've learned
i want to share with you, my daughter.
things i hope you remember
when your footsteps start to falter.

not one person is all good,
not one is all bad either.
this includes each one of us,
the saints, the thieves, the dreamers.

you don't have to obey or impress any man,
you don't need even one to approve.
you're every bit as capable (or more)
and dear, that's the god's honest truth.

at times you'll have to work quite hard
for everything you need
you may question the purpose of living,
just to struggle down on your knees?

but brighter days will come your way,
whether weeks or months or years.
not one thing lasts forever,
not sorrow, anger, or fear.

and though this means that joyful moments
will also come and pass,
there are ways to hold on to your peace,
there are ways to help it last.

look for the helpers, cherish the people
who truly accept who you are,
who hold you through your darkest journeys,
no matter how rocky or far.

for i will not always be with you,
the one truth i hate to reveal.
i know it's hard to think about,
a wound i wish i could heal.

but whether i'm here, or whether i'm gone,
there are truths that i hope you will hold.
you are the greatest joy of my life,
you are loving and worthy and bold.

you are stronger than your worst days,
you'll forever deserve your own grace.
and you are the one who taught me to love
the moment i first saw your face.

forever

i used to fear forever,
a long table with a bright light
at an end that never arrives.
(i longed for an ending.)

but now, forever
could never contain
enough sleepy mornings
waking in my love's soft embrace.

forever could never
provide enough evenings
holding his hand
in the warm summer breeze.

and now, forever
could never contain
enough slap-happy bedtime
giggles with my daughter.

forever could never
provide enough moments
to soak in the feeling
of her squeezing me tight.

and now i know there's
no reason to fear forever,
because forever will never occur,
(even if i've started to wish it would)

so i'll gather the ones
i love best in this life,
and i'll love them as hard as i can,
so they'll never forget.

and when the sun sets
on my tiny time here,
there will be no doubt
it was all worth it.

www.ingramcontent.com/pod-product-compliance
Lightning Source LLC
La Vergne TN
LVHW010844200726
843508LV00012B/2746